Pieces of My Heart

Irma Reyes Glidden

BookLeaf Publishing

India | USA | UK

Presentation by *BookLeaf Publishing*

Web: www.bookleafpub.com

E-mail: info@bookleafpub.com

ISBN: 9789358316278

First edition 2023

DEDICATION

To my Mom and Dad,

You will forever be my inspiration

for a full and happy life

Dad

The dampness of my hands
was gone
The moment I saw your smile, and your kind,
warm eyes
The moment you took mine
and walked me into the classroom
on my very first day of school.

The dampness of my hands
was gone
The moment you said, "easy on the gas, you can
do it, just slowly press your foot on the brake"
The moment I sat in the driver's seat for the first
time driving on the empty runway of the Naval
air base where we lived.

The dampness of my hands
was gone
the moment I witnessed you clasp yours together
to pump the beat back into that young sailor's
heart, a stranger...
hearing you beg with each compression, "Come
on son, come back, you can do this son!"
until his eyes opened and he gasped a breath of
life.

The dampness of my hands
was gone
The moment you secured my cap and brushed
the lint from my gown
The moment you clapped loudly with pride
during the pomp and circumstance
The moment you walked me down the aisle to
meet up with that young sailor, no longer a
stranger
And the moment you held your first born
grandson for the first time.

The dampness of my hands
was gone
The moment you taught me, "You are not rich
until you have something that money cannot
buy, which are the true gifts in life..
Integrity
Compassion
Respect
Happiness
Love
and most especially Time"

My hands were so damp
The moment I clasped them together
as I tried pumping the beat back into your
heart...

begging with each compression
"Come on Dad, come back, you can do this
Dad!"
Remembering with each compression
what you taught me about the gift of Time...
"Time is precious...and it slips away every
second of everyday. Never take it for granted
because once it passes, you can never get it
back"

My hands were so damp
every day for 70 days
as you lay silently sleeping
the machines regulating your
breath and your heart
Time was passing so slowly
refusing to let you go
because we want more Time

The dampness of my hands
was gone
the moment the greatest man I have ever known
held mine in his
as he took his final breath.

And then
The dampness of my hands
is gone.

Mom

The faded handwriting
the opaqueness of the paper
barely revealing
the inscription on the frail edges
folded neatly in every letter
the one simple phrase
"No Other Love"

Tears welled in my eyes
flowing easily as I choked up
reading mom's heart poured out
onto these old pages
Dad asking Mom to wait patiently
for his return from deployment
saying that Time will not pass fast enough
and yet

The length of Time matters not
What matters is
he has faith that the distance
does not break their bond or connection
nor their Love that transcends all Time
"I know this in my heart", he wrote
no matter how long it takes
and no matter how far apart they are
there is "No Other Love"

Sitting on the corner of their bed
Her face in her hands
Alone
The other half of her heart
lying in a hospital bed

Tears welled in my eyes
flowing easily as I choked up
She never left his side
Her hands entwined in his
Every day for 70 days
praying and singing softly
until the only man she ever loved
took his final breath

"Sleep peacefully now, hon
there is No Other Love"

Losing the other half of your heart
is a pain you never think you will survive
Heartbreaking is the sound
of someone crying in grief
because it's all you've been hearing
You know exactly what it sounds like
even in the silence of solitude
A cry that pierces your heart
and is like no other
until you find Peace

The doctors said six to twelve months
is all she may have left
End stage renal failure
The only thing I've ever wanted to fight
A new kidney will make you better
this is now your plight

I want to give you mine
since we match 100%
but your body is too tired and frail
and you may not survive

Please God, please give us more Time
I will give up everything to have more Time
She said she is ok and at peace
She will be with Dad the moment
her heart will cease

Tears welled in my eyes
flowing easily as I choked up
Six months and 17 days
was all the Time we were blessed
Heartbreaking is the sound
of someone crying in grief
A cry that pierces your heart
and is like no other
until you find Peace

Selfless and unassuming
Larger than life itself
Energetic and headstrong
Kind, yet iron-willed
Mom was unstoppable

A generous and thoughtful heart
Gave everything to us, her children
her grandchildren,
Family always came first
no matter how far apart
Her religion and faith was strong

Rest peacefully together now,
Mom and Dad
where your love transcends all Time
where there is
"No Other Love"

The Eldest

Born 15 months before me
perfectly suited to be the Eldest
always the straightest arrow
undeviating from your path
from Eagle Scout to
Your Honor

You are my favorite
My big brother

My pride in you
has been constant
always looking up to you
since the day I knew I was your
little sister

Tagging along
throughout every year in school
from K through Cal
Growing up working together
in very different but important positions
still always known as your
little sister

Your diagnosis was dire

End stage renal failure
The only thing I've ever wanted to fight
A new kidney will make you better
this is now your plight

I want to give you mine
since we match 100%
but there is another
just as sickly as you
our own loving Sister

Thank God for your donor
devastating for their family
yet a wonderful blessing for ours
So grateful for their selflessness

Because without you, big brother
Our family's strength
Would not be as powerful and solid
Without your tenacity and courage
We would falter
Thank you, big brother for
holding us all together

Sistar

Your excitement about this boy
brought us both laughter and joy
We read each card
to find the perfect one
"What about a gift?" you asked
"He's 15! Here, just put in this dollar"

Mom dressed us in identical outfits
though we are not twins
In fact, very much the opposite
much to mom's chagrin
Your shyness made me fiercely protective
over my delicate little sister

I taught you how to rollerskate
and dragged you to babysitting jobs
We lived on an island
Time and time again
I'd rescue you
because you could not swim
the swimming lessons
mom made us take
I loved every lesson
yet each one you would hate

Protecting you from the bullies
trying to shove you out of the way
at the plethora of Boy Band concerts
we could never miss, no way

Onkatonk
Baking cookies
Magic Cups
Makeup, Hair
and Photoshoots

Wonderful memories
flooded my mind
when told about your
very rare blood disease
only thirty eight people
in the World
and you are number thirty nine

Six weeks in the hospital
that boy never leaving your side
Dialysis every night
End stage renal failure
The only thing I've ever wanted to fight
A new kidney will make you better
this is now your plight

I want to give you mine
since we match 100%

but there is another
just as sickly as you
our own loving brother

Patiently you wait
Feeling weaker every day
that boy never leaving your side
Every day for many days, weeks
and years
Caring for and uplifting you
until finally
Thank God for your donor
we all collapsed in tears

Your excitement about this boy
remains the same
even almost 40 years later
No longer a boy,
and even a bit taller
given to that boy many years ago
This man still has that dollar

The Youngest

Your crooked smile is still the same,
funny, bright and contagious
Dad said we can't go to the beach
until you're awake
Wake up, little brother, wake up soon

You were dad's favorite
the Bunso

We arrived home
You pretending to sleep
so Dad could carry you to bed
your crooked smile gave you up
but Dad still cradled you
as you pretended to sleep
Wake up, little brother, wake up soon

You are my favorite
My little brother

I took care of you even until
you were no longer little
Fiercely protective of me
I secretly didn't mind when
you became the inquisitor

"Don't break my sister's heart"
told to each of my suitors

Your hand entwined with Dad's
standing aside his hospital bed
Every day for 70 days
Playing healing music
Praying it will work
Begging for him to
Wake up, Dad, please wake up soon

25% sibling was what your test revealed.
Did we even know what this meant?
It must be a mistake
you are our brother 100%
Let's all take the test
to prove it is a mistake

Heart pounding Bewilderment
that there was no mistake
The depth of love is not diminished
because of this mistake
Telling myself
this must be a dream and to
Wake up, please, please wake up soon

The hooks of denial
dig so deep
a secret 50 years to keep

Unrelenting to seek the truth
Who is your dad if he is not mine?
How can this be?
It must be a mistake

Yet...
There is another
The sister of my brother
Whose dad is his
But is not mine

Wake up, little brother, wake up soon

The First Born

My heart poured out
pounding so strong
Joyful tears streaming down
Your entire life
flashed before me
though you were not yet born

Your great grandfather's namesake
you proudly hold your name
From the moment you were born
Life was never the same

I worried about you
because you were my first
how can I raise this little person
I've never done this before
I've never been a mother
I feel so immersed

We still have a laugh
about you in third person
referring to yourself by your name
in your raspy little voice

I struggled and felt I deprived you

of an easy and good childhood
Single and alone
I didn't know how to teach you
Yet you still found your way

I was your champion and defender
Then you became mine
You taught me how to persevere
when it was just you and I

You remind me of me
still to this day
not settling
for something or someone not worthy
steadfast and without exception

You are grown up now
but in my eyes you will always be fifteen
just last week you were only fifteen

I was your champion and defender
and will forever and always be
no matter how grown up you are
and taller you are than me

I am proud of the man
that you have become
but mostly I am so proud
that you are my son

Little Bear

Intelligent and insightful
Actually more Genius
you taught yourself
to master all things
you make everything seemless

Not one worry
have you ever given me
since the day you were born
Stress-free and easy
You learned on your own

From Reading to Chess
Golf, real and mini
Football, Basketball
and even Bowling
Endless feats and achievements

I never had to push you
Born with ambition
you excel in all things
and bring all things to fruition

Always so Thoughtful and Kind
Courageous and Humble

with Unwavering Integrity
deserving of all the Respect
you've been receiving

You are grown up now
but in my eyes you will always be twelve
Just last week you were only twelve

I am proud of the man
that you have become
but mostly I am so proud
that you are my son

Mylene

I don't know what I would do
without you
You have been our Angel
We could not have survived without you

You were the best thing that happened
to my little brother
We became fast friends
Then you became our family
and I can't imagine our family without you

You said you were weak
and struggled to go on
every year a profound loss
yet you were the sanity
that escaped me
the strength you thought
was long gone

Even in your darkest moments
Your light shone bright
on our family
Your strength strong enough
to carry all of us
We could not have survived without you

Waking early every morning
Staying up late every night
Rarely getting a break
Preparing every meal
and medicine
not only for mom, but for your family
I don't know what I'd do without you

You carried your burdens silently
not to show strength
just exhausted on all levels
Physical, Mental, and Emotional
Yet even with these burdens
You are the strongest woman I know
We could not have survived without you

I love you more than you can imagine.

James

You cared for my little sister
since you were fifteen
high school sweethearts
you knew it would last
beyond the wisdom of youth
the years moving fast

Unexpected illness
making her frail
You stood by her side
as everything derailed

Her illness so rare
you knew not what to do
yet you stood by her side
to pull her through

Coming out of the dark
took months and years
A lot of pain and anguish
and a lot of tears

Through it all
you accepted the challenge
never giving up

on my little sister

Since you were fifteen
Your love for her so strong
At first you were the boy
afraid to call her
Then you became the
Man who saved the dollar

Susan

Even though at first we didn't
see eye to eye
Clashing on unimportant matters
we had to at least try

The spouse of the Eldest
is not an easy role
But you took it head on
And had everything in control

Especially when we needed you most
You came through for us
First when we lost dad
You kept us together
We couldn't even
Navigate our daily lives
You became our tether

Then when we lost mom
You became the Rock
for my brother
and you both the Backbone
for our family
I cannot imagine it without you

Always Elegant and Graceful
Your head held high
still sometimes not seeing
eye to eye
Yet that matters not
What matters is
You are my sister and I love you

Adam

I watched silently from the corner
you were trying to be strong,
you were so strong
I didn't see any tears
as you clutched the front of your jacket
near your heart

You are my favorite
My first born nephew

I watched silently from the corner, your persed
lips began to tremble
you didn't know anyone was watching
you were holding your breath
saying your final goodbye
it was your own moment

I witnessed your raw emotion
your tears freely flowing
Never seeing it before this day
It traveled to my silent corner

Tears welled in my eyes
flowing easily as I choked up
I felt connected to you
in this heartbroken yet beautiful way

Junior

The only son of my sister
you filled her heart with love
You kept her youthful and active
Playing games and Singing
Shopping, Cooking
Work and school
All of the above

You couldn't say Junior
so I call you Noona
You are my favorite,
my wonderful nephew

An only child of my sister
She didn't imagine
the joy you'd return to her
You uplift and inspire her

You struggled when she got sick
You knew not what to do
You held her hand and made her smile
Whenever she felt blue

That was all she needed
that special love from you

her one and only son
As long as you were there
her battle was already won

Take care of your mother
my one and only little sister
The comfort and joy you bring her
can never be matched by another

Princess

My dear niece, so full of grace
The title Grandpa gave you
belonged to me first
But when you were born
I knew I'd have to relinquish it
I willingly did at Grandpa's request
because I knew you would carry it best

My beautiful niece,
You are my favorite

Your beauty resonates like your mother's light
and you take after my brother's might
But it's your own brilliance, so outstanding
That propels you forward, dreams expanding

Imaginative and bright,
nothing holds you back
You chase your goals,
determined in your track
So my dear Princess, without a doubt
You are cherished, beyond words
throughout

Marlene

Oldest daughter
of my youngest brother
you remind me of me
when I was a young mother

My beautiful niece,
You are my favorite

You entered our lives
Wide eyed and sweet
now this little Joy of your own
makes your circle complete

It never made sense before
when you are told,
"The depth of your love
is never known
until you have
children of your own"

You never knew
how much love
your heart could hold
until the day your child
you behold

The truth of this is profound
for the rest of your life
You are no longer important
your heart will melt
and your love will be felt
by this little Joy of your own

Gabe

The curtain opened
not knowing what to expect
our first attendance
at your first performance

You are my favorite,
my talented nephew

Our mouths and eyes wide open
in unbelievable awe
who even knew
this talent you grew

You belted your heart out
with your magical voice
your lines delivered meticulously
you rejoice

Our hearts pounding in excitement
with each and every scene
My nephew, "Jack Kelly"
a powerful force

You found your passion
it cannot be denied

we had no idea
this amazing gift
you have inside

The rumble of the clapping
the stomping in the thrill
the theater was impassioned
no one could stay still

Your amazing smile
was wide and bright
during the curtain call
the entire audience
screaming in delight

So proud of you
and your genius flair
my brilliant nephew
high is where you set the bar
never stop reaching
for the stars

Ryan

My youngest nephew
you are special indeed
Expectations of your
accomplishments
You did exceed

The middle child, humble and wise
A quiet strength that never wavers
With intelligence and cleverness
You achieve all your endeavors

You are my favorite,
my youngest nephew

Oh, how lovely it is
To see my nephew grow
Unique and special
With talents that truly show

My youngest nephew shines
Surpassing expectations, it's true
His accomplishments, so bright
A talented spirit, through and through
You hold a special place
In my heart, forever true

The Twins

"Your twins look just like you!
So adorable"
Strangers would say
The three of us would just smile
and say Thank You
The daughters of my brother
No need for them to know
I am your Aunt and not your Mother

The day I found out
two of you there were
Tears of joy I could not contain
it seemed all a happy blur
So tiny and precious
You melted my heart
you're the daughters I never had
and we'd never be far apart

Crooked little smiles
just like your dad
your laughter so infectious

Goofy like your mom
with your silly and funny dances
More tomboy than girlie

just like me, your proud Auntie

Grandpa's little Princetitas
Please don't grow up
Please stay tiny and precious
My beautiful weekend daughters

My Love

He said it's been almost a year
Yet it's been only three months
He said Love, it feels longer
It hasn't been that long
He said I'd swear it was at least 10 months
We just grew close to each other so quickly
since it's been only three months
He said then it hasn't been long enough, Love

The length of Time matters not
What matters is
The quality and depth of our connection
The rarity of our special bond
The comfort and fulfillment in our hearts
The balance, peace, and closeness felt when
we're together, and even when we're apart
The Love that transcends all Time

He said I adore your family
Because he's never known the same with his
own
Yet it's been only four months
He said I Love your family
It melted my heart
He said the crash after the happiness

fills him with longing and sadness
Because he's never felt the same with his own
I AM your family
He said No, Love, You Are Not, it hasn't been
that long
It's been only four months
It hasn't been long enough, Love

The length of time matters not
What matters is
You were welcomed warmly and without
prejudice
into my close-knit and loving family
Without the length of time as a prerequisite
because it matters not
What matters is
My family knew you were important enough to
me to include you in ours
That I held you in high regard, respect & trust
you with my heart
That is why they embraced you, Love
not because Time has been long enough

Time stood still for just a moment,
His hand softly caressing my face
His tender gaze calming and slowing my breath
Time was frozen for that moment
and there was no one else but us
It feels more than long enough

The length of time matters not
What matters is
We may never get the chance for it to be long
enough
Time is a priceless and precious gift
We always think we have more Time,
that Time is infinite and we can wait until it has
been long enough

The length of time matters not
What matters is
What we do with that gift of Time
We are never promised any more Time
than what we have Today
We always only have Today
Even when tomorrow comes
It will be Today

Even if Time is frozen
It will still always be Today
Don't wait for long enough to happen
Because you may never have a chance to reach it

The length of time matters not
What matters is
Today is priceless
Today is a gift
Today is already long enough

All of You

You've been through the same sorrow
My strong and wonderful family
My heart shattered into a million pieces
I fumbled in the dark
to put the pieces back together

Grief is very personal and different for everyone
The weight of our loss was crushing
The pain feels like something we could not
survive

Though the pieces still broken
each of you shined
your wonderful light on me
You sent Healing and Loving energy
and helped me find the pieces
of my shattered heart

I'm slowly putting them back together
My heart will never be completely whole
but having each of you in my life brings it closer
each day

I love all of you
more than there are
words to describe it